dabblelab

SOCK PUPPET THEATER PRESENTS

Little Red Riding Hood

A Make and Play Production

by Christopher L. Harbo

CAPSTONE PRESS
a capstone imprint

Dabble Lab Books are published by Capstone Press,
1710 Roe Crest Drive, North Mankato, Minnesota 56003
www.mycapstone.com

Cataloging-in-Publication Data is available at the Library of Congress website.
ISBN: 978-1-5157-6680-3 (library binding)
ISBN: 978-1-5157-6684-1 (eBook PDF)

Editorial Credits

Juliette Peters, designer; Marcy Morin, puppet and prop creator;
Sarah Schuette, photo stylist; Morgan Walters, media researcher;
Tori Abraham, production specialist

Photo Credits

All photos by Capstone Studio, Karon Dubke with the exception of Shutterstock: Andy Dean Photography, 26, 29, Bildagentur Zoonar GmbH, 5, Eric Isselee, 4, Mammut Vision, design element throughout, Pattern image, design element throughout, photocell, design element throughout, structuresxx, 21, 22-23, 24-25, Yomka, design element throughout

Printed in Canada.
010395F17

About the Author

Christopher L. Harbo grew up watching *Sesame Street*, *Mister Rogers' Neighborhood*, and *The Muppet Show*. Ever since then, he's wanted to be a puppeteer — and now his dream has finally come true! In addition to puppetry, Christopher enjoys folding origami, reading comic books, and watching superhero movies.

Table of Contents

Little Red Riding Hood

The most popular version of *Little Red Riding Hood* dates back to the 1800s. Titled "Little Red Cap," it was published in German by the Brothers Grimm. Since then the tale has been retold in countless books, TV shows, and movies.

Now you can bring Little Red Riding Hood's story to life. The pages that follow are overflowing with creative ideas for building and performing a complete sock puppet production. You'll find simple instructions for making the puppets, stage, and props. You'll also discover a full play script and helpful performance tips. So what are you waiting for? It's time to try your hand at puppeteering!

The Plot

The fairy tale begins with a young girl receiving a red cloak from her mother. Her mom then asks Little Red Riding Hood to take food to her sick grandmother, warning her not to stop along the way.

As Red travels, a hungry wolf sees her walking through the woods. The wolf asks Red where she is headed, and she tells him. The wolf suggests that some freshly picked flowers might cheer up her grandmother, so Red stops to collect a bouquet.

Meanwhile, the wolf uses the delay to race to grandmother's house. He quickly eats Red's grandma, puts on her nightcap, and takes her place in bed. When Red finally arrives, she thinks her grandma looks and sounds odd. Realizing the jig is up, the wolf leaps up and eats the girl.

Soon a woodcutter arrives and discovers what has happened. He quickly cuts open the wolf's belly. He saves Red and her grandma, who are still alive in the wolf's stomach. Then the woodcutter crams stones into the wolf's belly and drowns him.

The Cast

Red

Little Red Riding Hood is a loving child who simply wants to please her grandma. Unfortunately, she is a little too trusting. She doesn't realize there are wolves in world that are up to no good.

Wolf

The sly old wolf is a smooth talker. He has all the right words to get just about anyone to trust him. But this nasty villain is only interested in a free lunch — and Red and her grandma are on the menu.

Woodcutter

The woodcutter is a brave, bearded fellow with a knack for sensing trouble. Lucky for Red and Granny, his instincts serve him well. With his life-saving know-how, the woodcutter becomes a hero.

Granny

Red's grandma is a kind old woman who lives all alone in the forest. She doesn't get many visitors — which may explain why she falls prey to the wolf's knock-knock joke. In the end, however, Granny proves she is tougher than she looks.

Sock Puppet Creation

Oh, you can call me Red.

Supplies to Create
Little Red Riding Hood

- large tan sock
- 3.25-inch (8.3-cm) foam half ball
- cardboard
- pencil
- scissors
- craft glue
- ruler
- brown yarn
- googly eyes
- tan craft foam
- pink felt
- dinner plate
- red fabric
- red cord
- small safety pin

5

1. Turn the sock inside out.

2. Place the flat side of the foam half ball on the cardboard. Trace around the base of the ball with a pencil.

3. Cut out the circle traced on the cardboard.

4. Fold the cardboard circle in half.

5. Glue one side of the folded cardboard to the base of the foam half ball. Line up the curve of the cardboard with the curved edge of the ball. The loose flap of cardboard will form the mouth of the puppet.

6. Apply glue to the inside of the top and bottom of the mouth. Tuck the toe of the sock into the mouth and allow the glue to dry.

7. Turn the sock right side out, pulling it over the foam half ball. Set aside to dry.

8. Cut 15 20-inch- (51-centimeter-) long pieces of yarn. Group them lengthwise on the table. Tie all 15 pieces together about 2 inches (5 cm) from one end.

9. Separate the long strands of loose yarn into three groups. Braid the groups until only 3 inches (7.6 cm) of yarn remain. Tie off the braid. Trim the loose yarn so it is even on both ends of the braid.

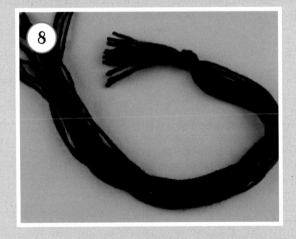

10. Glue the hair across the top of the puppet's head.

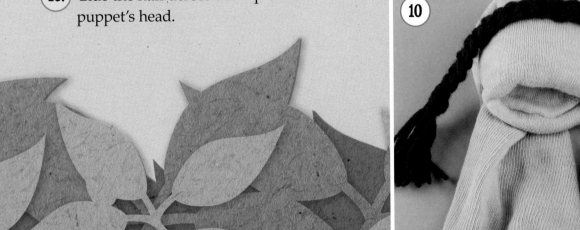

11. Glue googly eyes to the puppet's head.

12. Cut a small nose out of the craft foam. Glue it below the eyes.

13. Cut a small half-moon shape out of pink felt. Glue it inside the mouth to form a tongue.

14. Place a dinner plate upside down on the backside of the red fabric. Trace around the plate with a pencil.

15. Cut out the circle traced on the fabric.

16. Cut an 8-inch- (20-cm-) long piece of cord. Glue it along the edge of the fabric's front side. Note that the cord does not go all the way around the fabric.

17. Place the fabric on the puppet's head to form a cape. Adjust so the edge with the cord runs along the top and behind the puppet's hair. Glue in place.

18. Gather the sides of the cape around the front of the puppet. Fasten the sides together under the mouth with a safety pin.

19. Cut a short piece of cord. Tie it in a bow to hide the safety pin and complete Little Red Riding Hood.

Big Bad Wolf

- utility knife
- 2-inch (5-cm) foam egg
- cardboard
- pencil
- 3.25-inch (8.3-cm) foam half ball
- 2 1-inch (2.5-cm) foam balls
- large gray sock
- scissors
- white craft foam
- craft glue
- gray felt
- hot glue
- gray faux fur
- googly eyes
- black pipe cleaner

Hello, hello, hello! Who do we have here?

1. With an adult's help, use a utility knife to cut the foam egg in half the long way.

2. Place the flat sides of the foam egg halves on the cardboard. Line them up so the wide ends are touching, back-to-back. Trace around the base of both egg halves with a pencil.

3. Cut out the cardboard egg shapes, but leave the two shapes connected where they meet.

4. Glue the cardboard egg shapes to the flat sides of the egg halves. Fold the egg halves toward each other until they meet to form one whole egg. The top half will serve as the upper jaw. The bottom half will serve as the lower jaw.

5. With an adult's help, hot glue the wide end of the upper jaw to the foam half ball. The flat side of the ball and the flat side of the upper jaw should line up. Once attached, the bottom jaw should be free to swing up and down.

6. Hot glue the two small foam balls side-by-side to the top of the foam half ball. This shape is the completed headpiece.

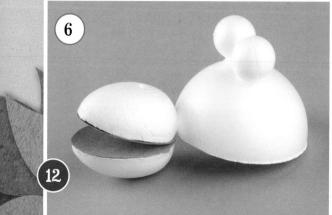

7. Slide the headpiece into the sock until the mouth stops at the end of the toe.

8. Pinch the sock's toe together between the upper and lower jaw. With an adult's help, hot glue the pinched fabric in place.

9. Cut out four pointy foam teeth. Glue two on either side of the mouth.

10. Cut two ear shapes out of the faux fur. Set aside.

11. Cut two smaller ear shapes out of the gray felt. Glue the gray inner ears to the faux fur outer ears.

12. Glue the completed ears to the puppet's head.

13. Glue googly eyes to the two bumps in the sock created by the foam balls on the headpiece.

14. Cut a short piece of pipe cleaner and bend it into a V-shape. Glue it above the eyes to finish the wolf puppet.

I always knew you had a good head on your shoulders.

Supplies to Create
Granny

- large tan sock
- 2 3.25-inch (8.3-cm) foam half balls
- cardboard
- pencil
- scissors
- craft glue
- curly faux hair
- googly eyes
- pink craft foam
- pink felt
- utility knife
- white fabric
- white lace
- large patterned sock
- 2 buttons
- toy glasses (optional)

1. Turn the tan sock inside out.

2. Place the flat side of the foam half ball on the cardboard. Trace around the base of the ball with a pencil.

3. Cut out the circle traced on the cardboard.

4. Fold the cardboard circle in half.

5. Glue one side of the folded cardboard to the base of the foam half ball. Line up the curve of the cardboard with the curved edge of the ball. The loose flap of cardboard will form the mouth of the puppet.

6. Apply glue to the inside of the top and bottom of the mouth. Tuck the toe of the sock into the mouth and allow the glue to dry.

7. Turn the sock right side out, pulling it over the foam half ball. Set aside to dry.

8. Cut short lengths of the faux hair and glue it to the top of the puppet's head.

9. Glue googly eyes to the puppet's head.

10. Cut a small nose out of the craft foam. Glue it below the eyes.

11. Cut a small half-moon shape out of pink felt. Glue it inside the mouth to form a tongue. Set the puppet aside.

12. Ask an adult to hollow out the underside of the remaining foam half ball with a utility knife.

13. Glue white fabric on top of the foam half ball. Trim off any extra fabric around the base of the ball.

14. Line the base of the half ball with lace. Glue in place and trim off any excess. Set the completed nightcap aside.

15. Cut the toe off the patterned sock. Slide the sock onto the puppet's body to serve as a nightgown.

16. Glue two buttons to the front of the nightgown.

17. Place the nightcap and glasses on the puppet's head to finish Granny.

Supplies to Create the
Woodcutter

- large tan sock
- 3.25-inch (8.3-cm) foam half ball
- cardboard
- pencil
- scissors
- craft glue
- googly eyes
- tan craft foam
- pink felt
- faux fur
  - gray craft foam
  - red craft foam
    - white craft foam
    - large plaid sock

Me thinks I hear the cry of a damsel in distress!

11

1. Turn the tan sock inside out.

2. Place the flat side of the foam half ball on the cardboard. Trace around the base of the ball with a pencil.

3. Cut out the circle traced on the cardboard.

4. Fold the cardboard circle in half.

5. Glue one side of the folded cardboard to the base of the foam half ball. Line up the curve of the cardboard with the curved edge of the ball. The loose flap of cardboard will form the mouth of the puppet.

6. Apply glue to the inside of the top and bottom of the mouth. Tuck the toe of the sock into the mouth and allow the glue to dry.

7. Turn the sock right side out, pulling it over the foam half ball. Set aside to dry.

8. Glue googly eyes to the puppet's head.

9. Cut a small nose out of the tan craft foam. Glue it below the eyes.

10. Cut a small half-moon shape out of pink felt. Glue it inside the mouth to form a tongue.

11. Cut a beard shape out of the faux fur. Cut a hole in the beard for the mouth. Glue the beard around the puppet's mouth.

12. Cut a small axe handle out of tan craft foam.

13. Cut a small axe blade out of gray craft foam.

14. Glue the axe blade to the handle. Add details to the blade with the red and white craft foam if you like.

15. Cut the toe off the plaid sock. Slide the sock onto the puppet's body to serve as a shirt.

16. Glue the axe to the plaid shirt to finish the woodcutter.

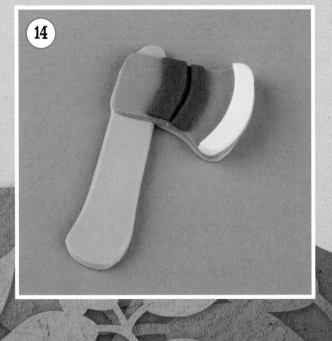

17

Stage and Prop Creation

Suggested Supplies:

- utility knife
- tri-fold display board
- wooden dowel
- curtain
- scissors
- beige felt
- brown felt
- craft glue
- white craft foam
- black marker
- tan felt
- fake flowers
- craft jewel
- cardboard
- craft sticks
- miniature basket
- fabric scraps

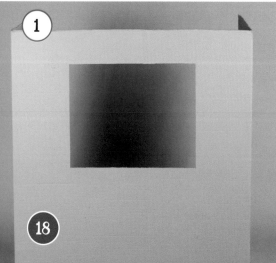

Stage:

1. Ask an adult to use a utility knife to cut a large rectangle out of the center of a tri-fold display board.

2. Cut holes near the top of the tri-fold board's side flaps. Slide a wooden dowel through one hole, a curtain, and then the second hole to make a simple backdrop.

Consider decorating the front of your stage with paint, tree branches, fake leaves, and fake flowers!

Granny's House:

1. Cut a rectangle out of beige felt and a trapezoid out of brown felt. Glue the trapezoid to the rectangle to make a house shape.

2. Cut windows and a door out of brown felt. Glue them to the front of the house.

3. Cut two smaller window shapes out of white craft foam. Glue them to the brown windows. Then use a black marker to draw window panes on the white foam.

4. Cut small trapezoids out of tan felt. Glue them under the windows to make window boxes. Glue fake flowers to the window boxes. Glue a craft gem to the door to make a doorknob.

5. Glue a small piece of cardboard to the back of the house for stability. Then glue a craft stick to the back of the house, near the bottom, to compete the prop.

19

Red's Basket:

1. Glue a fabric scrap to the top of a miniature basket. Cut a small slit in the fabric to allow fake flowers to slide into the basket.

2. Glue a craft stick to the back of the basket to complete the prop.

Granny's Bed:

1. Use a scissors to cut two long strips of cardboard. These will be the sideboards of the bed.

2. Cut a large headboard shape out of cardboard. Then cut a smaller footboard shape out of cardboard.

3. Glue the sideboards to the headboard and footboard to create a simple bed shape. The middle of the bed will be open to allow Granny and the wolf to slide in and out.

4. Use scraps of fabric to make blankets and even a pillow to complete your bed prop.

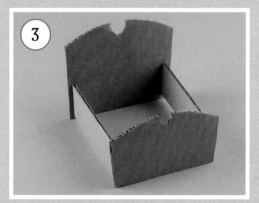

Now that the stage is set, it's time to read the script!

The Script

Narrator:	Once upon a time, Little Red Riding Hood set out with a basket of goodies to visit her grandma deep in the forest.
Red:	*(skipping on stage with empty basket)* La la la! What a fine day for a stroll in the woods.
Narrator:	Not long after she entered the deep, dark woods, a wolf spied the young girl skipping along the path.
Wolf:	*(poking head in from curtain, speaking to audience)* Hmm . . . Me thinks dinner is served! *(ducks back behind curtain)*
Red:	La la la!
Wolf:	*(pops up in front of Red)* Hello, hello, hello! Who do we have here?
Red:	Oh, my! You startled me, Mr. Wolf. It is just me, Little Red Riding Hood.
Wolf:	And where might you be going today, Ms. Hood?
Red:	Oh, you can call me Red. I'm off to deliver this basket of goodies to my granny.
Wolf:	Your granny! Well, aren't you a savory — I mean sweet — little girl.

Wolf: *(turns to speak to audience)* Ha, ha! If I play this right, I'll get two meals for the price of one! *(turns back to Red)*

Red: *(looks at audience, then at wolf, confused)* Were you saying something, Mr. Wolf?

Wolf: Not at all, Red. Not at all. But if you don't mind me asking, where does your delicious — I mean dear — granny live?

Red: At the very end of this path, deep in the forest. Her house is really quite easy to find.

Wolf: You don't say?! In that case, may I offer a suggestion, Red?

Red: Of course, Mr. Wolf.

Wolf: It looks like the only thing you're missing is a nice bouquet of flowers to go with that basket of goodies. Why not pick a few pansies to go with your pastries?

Red: That's a great idea! My granny just loves flowers!

Red: *(looks left and right)* And what luck! I see a nice patch of flowers right over there. *(walks offstage with basket)*

Narrator: And so, Little Red Riding Hood left the path to gather a big bunch of flowers. Meanwhile, the crafty wolf darted down the path, straight to her grandma's house.

Wolf: *(running)* Ho, ho! I can't believe Red fell for it. While she picks flowers, I'll get to Granny's house ahead of her.

Wolf: *(house pops up on stage)* And look, there it is now!

Wolf: *(walks up to house)* Knock. Knock.

Granny: *(pops up behind house)* Who's there?

Wolf: Eaton.

Granny: *(comes around to front of house)* Eaton who?

Wolf: Eaton you for dinner! Now get in my tummy! *(charges Granny)*

Granny: EEK! *(both duck below stage)*

Wolf: *(offstage)* CHOMP! CHOMP! GOBBLE! GOBBLE! GULP!

Narrator: With grandma snug in his tummy, the wolf put on her nightgown, jumped in her bed, and waited for Little Red Riding Hood to arrive.

Narrator: *(Red walks on stage with basket of flowers)* Before long, the little girl came upon the house. Much to her surprise, Granny was not there to greet her.

Red: Oh dear! Where's Granny? She always meets me at the front door. Yoo-hoo! Granny! Are you in there?

Wolf: *(high pitched voice, from offstage)* Hello, dear. I'm not feeling well today. Come in so I can eat — I mean greet — you properly.

Narrator: Little Red Riding Hood entered the house and walked into her grandma's bedroom. *(house pops down and Wolf in bed rises up)*

Red: Hello, Granny. You really are under the weather. You don't sound like yourself today. In fact, you don't look quite right either.

Wolf: Why, whatever do you mean, my treat — I mean — sweet?

Red: Well, for starters, what big ears you have!

Wolf: The better to hear you with, my dear.

Red: And Granny, what big eyes you have!

Wolf: The better to see you with, my dear.

Red: But grandma, what big teeth you have!

Wolf: *(with regular wolf voice)* The better to eat you with, my dear! *(wolf jumps up and charges toward Red)* Now get in my tummy and join your granny!

Red: AHHH! HELP! A big bad wolf is trying to eat me! *(throws basket of flowers at wolf)*

Narrator:	As luck would have it, a woodcutter passing by Granny's house heard Red's cry.
Woodcutter:	*(pops in from side)* Me thinks I hear the cry of a damsel in distress! *(ducks back out)*
Narrator:	Not wasting another moment, the woodcutter burst through the front door and stepped between the wolf and the little girl.
Woodcutter:	*(pops up between Red and wolf)* Hold it right there, bub. Just what do you think you're doing?
Wolf:	Stand aside, mister. Granny's tucked in my tummy. Now I intend to gobble up Red as a bedtime snack.
Woodcutter:	Not if my Head-butt Heimlich Maneuver has anything to say about it. *(rams headfirst into the wolf's stomach)*
Sound Effect:	BONK!

Wolf:	BLECH! *(bends over, throwing up)*
Red:	*(up pops Granny)* Granny! You're alive!
Wolf:	*(turning to audience)* This is awkward.
Granny:	Thank you, Charles. I always knew you had a good head on your shoulders.
Woodcutter:	Glad to help, Mabel. Now let's go see what Red's got in that basket of hers. *(all three walk offstage — leaving the wolf behind)*
Wolf:	*(looking at the audience)* BURP! I don't feel so good. *(walks offstage in the opposite direction)*

The End

Take the Stage!

Are your puppets, props, and stage ready? Do you and your friends know all of the characters' lines? If so, you're almost ready for the big show. But before you give a live performance, consider these tips to make it the best it can be.

Create Voices

Just as no two people sound the same, none of your puppets should sound exactly alike either. Give your characters voices that seem natural to them. For example, maybe Red has a soft, kind voice while the woodcutter has a strong, burly voice. Meanwhile, the wolf might have a growly voice and Granny may have a weak, crackly voice.

Develop Personalities

Your puppets' personalities are as important as their voices. Look for ways to show the audience who your characters are through their actions, movements, and dialogue. Here are a few fun ideas to play with:

• The wolf is a smooth talker when he meets Red in the forest. As they speak, let him glide from one side of her to the other. His fluid motions will match his convincing voice.

• When Red arrives at her grandma's house, she is confused by the way her "grandma" looks. Consider having Red do a double-take — look at the wolf, then at the audience, and then back at the wolf — to help show her confusion.

• The woodcutter plays the hero in this story. Allow him to pop on stage dramatically and stand taller than the wolf. Giving him a strong posture will match his heroic nature.

Plan Your Movements

During the play, the puppets will need to move in and out of scenes and across the stage. Decide ahead of time what each one should do and when. For instance, how will the wolf run to Granny's house? Should he hop up and down or swerve back and forth across the stage? And how should the woodcutter launch his attack on the wolf? Should it happen fast or in slow motion? The choice is yours!

Practice the Play

The secret to every great performance is practice, practice, practice. Take time to run through your play more than once before performing it.

A round of rehearsals will help make your puppet show a hit!

The Show Must Go On!

You've performed *Little Red Riding Hood* and your show was a smashing success! While you could pack up your puppets, now is the time to really get creative. Try these ideas for reinventing your play and having even more fun with your creations:

Continue the story. What happens to Red, Granny, or the woodcutter after the wolf leaves? Does Red encounter the wolf on her walk back home? The possibilities are endless!

Give each of the characters superpowers. What would happen if Red could fly, the wolf had super-speed, Granny had super-strength, and the woodcutter had X-ray vision?

Create a new setting for your play. What would happen if Red's granny lived in a big city instead of a forest? Imagine the ways it might change the story and the roles of some of the characters.

Change the ending. What would happen if the wolf gobbled up Red before the woodcutter arrived? Would he still save her, or would the wolf get away? Give your tale's ending an unexpected twist.

Conclusion

Now that you've mastered *Little Red Riding Hood*, what comes next? Luckily there are hundreds of fables, fairy tales, and myths to make into puppet shows. Pick a story you like and be creative. Your next great sock puppet performance is at your fingertips!

Glossary

audience (AW-dee-uhns)—people who watch or listen to a play, movie, or show

character (KAYR-ik-tuhr)—a person or creature in a story

damsel (DAM-zuhl)—a young woman

dialogue (DYE-uh-lawg)—the words spoken between two or more characters

distress (di-STRES)—in urgent need of help

faux (FOH)—made to look like something else through an artistic effect

Heimlich maneuver (HIME-lik muh-NOO-ver)—a safety procedure used to help someone who is choking

performance (pur-FOR-muhnss)—the public presentation of a play, movie, or piece of music

personality (pur-suh-NAL-uh-tee)—all of the qualities or traits that make one person different from others

posture (POSS-chur)—the position of your body

production (pruh-DUHK-shuhn)—a play or any form of entertainment that is presented to others

prop (PROP)—an item used by an actor or performer during a show

rehearsal (ri-HURSS-uhl)—a practice performance of a script

savory (SAY-vuh-ree)—pleasing to the taste or smell

script (SKRIPT)—the story for a play, movie, or television show

trapezoid (TRAP-uh-zoid)—a four-sided shape that only has one set of parallel sides

Read More

Kandel, Tiger, and Heather Schloss. *The Ultimate Sock Puppet Book: Clever Tips, Tricks, and Techniques for Creating Imaginative Sock Puppets.* Minneapolis: Creative Publishing International, 2014.

Petelinsek, Kathleen. *Making Sock Puppets.* How-to Library. Ann Arbor, Mich.: Cherry Lake Publishing, 2015.

Reynolds, Toby. *Making Puppets.* Mini Artist. New York: Windmill Books, 2016.

Internet Sites

Use FactHound to find Internet sites related to this book.

Visit *www.facthound.com*

Just type in 9781515766803 and go.

 Check out projects, games and lots more at
www.capstonekids.com

Maker Space Tips

Download tips and tricks for using this book and others in a library maker space.

Visit *www.capstonepub.com/dabblelabresources*

TITLES IN THIS SET: